Admiral Zheng He:

The Collaborative

Transformational Expert

(This article is extracted from the book,

"Ancient Chinese Wisdom To Transform

Your Business: Lessons from Zheng He,

Confucius and Sun Zi")

Author: Dr. Michael Teng

Published in 2014 by

Corporate Turnaround Centre Pte Ltd.

About the Author: Dr Michael Teng

Where was he born? When? Where did he go to school etc?

He has a Doctor of Business Administration (DBA) degree from the University of South Australia, and a Master of Business Administration (MBA), and Bachelor of Mechanical Engineering (BENG) from the National University of Singapore. He is also a Professional Engineer (P Eng, Singapore), Chartered Engineer (C Eng, UK), and Fellow Member of several prestigious professional institutes, namely Chartered Institute of Marketing (FCIM), Chartered Management Institute (FCMI), Institute of Mechanical Engineers (FIMechE), Marketing Institute of Singapore (FMIS), and Institute of Electrical Engineers (FIEE); he is a Senior Member of Singapore Computer Society (SMSCS). He is also a Practicing Management Consultant (PMC) certified by the Singapore government.

Dr. Teng is widely recognized by the news media

as a turnaround CEO in Asia. His subject of interest is corporate turnaround and transformation, as well as internet marketing. He has been, on many occasions, interviewed by the international media such as Malaysian Business Radio, BFM 89-9, News Radio FM 93.8, Malaysian Business Radio, Edge Radio (USA), the Channel News Asia, *The Boss Magazine*, *Economic Bulletin*, the *Today*, *World Executive Digest*, Lianhe ZaoPao, StarBiz, and the *Straits Times*. His online seminars are broadcast in 120 countries via Success University and Skyquest.Com.

Dr. Mike Teng is the author of a best-selling book *Corporate Turnaround: Nursing a Sick Company Back to Health* published in 2002. The book was translated into Bahasa, Indonesia and Mandarin and was endorsed by both management guru Professor Philip Kotler and business tycoons Mr. Oei Hong Leong and Dr. YY Wong. Dr. Teng has subsequently authored more than twenty five management books.

What is unique with his books?

A man of universal/regional/continental renown: Dr. Teng is appointed by the Singapore government as the national trainer to coach and instruct displaced senior managers and deploy them to run SMEs.

He has more than 29 years of experience in corporate turnaround and transformation, engaging in strategic planning and handling operational management responsibilities in the Asia Pacific region. In these areas of expertise, he has held positions such as Chief Executive Officer for 20 years in multi-national and publicly listed companies. He was the CEO of a U.S. MNC based in Singapore for ten years. He spearheaded the turnaround of several troubled companies. He also advised several boards of directors of publicly listed companies.

Dr. Teng served as an Executive Council member for fourteen years and the last four years as the President of the Marketing Institute of Singapore (2000 – 2004), the national marketing association. He is the Chairman of the Chartered Management Institute (UK), Singapore branch, President of the National University of Singapore, MBA Alumni and past President of the University of South Australia.

Admiral Zheng He: The Collaborative Transformation Expert

China's greatest transformation expert was, arguably, Admiral Zheng He. Zheng He (also transliterated as "Cheng Ho") served the Ming Dynasty's Emperor Yongle (Zhu Di) and Yongle's grandson, Emperor XuanZong, as an overseas ambassador. Long famous as a diplomat, Zheng He may also serve as an example of a collaborative business executive who utilized the three phases of corporate transformation.

In contrast to autocratic monarchs or "lone wolf" chief executives, Zheng He exemplified collaboration even when seeking a goal with single-minded determination. This article also examines how Jack Welch, the former CEO of General Electric and renowned transformational manager also used collaborative efforts to bring GE to greater heights six hundred years later. He also mellowed down his style as a Neutron Jack in the earlier years of his career to Transformational Jack, following the footsteps of Zheng He's art of collaboration.

Zheng He is a Role Model for Modern China

China's current and past leaders consider Zheng He a pivotal example and praised him highly. Hu Jintao, the President said: "In the 15th century, the Ming Dynasty sent Zheng He to Australia and contributed greatly to the economy of Australia". Wen Jiabao, the Prime Minister said: "Zheng He was a great diplomat. All his voyages were to bring friendship, wealth, gifts and technology to benefit the countries that he visited. The Chinese are indeed kind and magnanimous." Jiang Zemin, President (1993 -2003) said: "Zheng He's voyages were very impressive. They showed that the Chinese people were trying to make friends with their neighbours and interact with them for mutual economic and cultural benefits. These resulted in the rapid progress of the world." Even the father of modern-day China, Deng Xiaoping, the paramount leader of the communist party said: "Zheng He demonstrated that China needs to be open. The Ming Dynasty was one of the more prosperous era in Chinese history because of Zheng He opening up China to the world."

History showed that after Zheng He, China was on

the path of decline until it started to open up again. It is not surprising that modern-day China which is the second largest economy in the world has continued to adopt Zheng He's spirit of diplomacy and adventurism.

Zheng He had served the Ming dynasty: a very prosperous time in China's history. His trade missions opened China to business opportunities with foreigners; after his death China closed in on itself. Modern Chinese economics seem to follow Zheng He's game plan by returning to international Asian markets. China has extended its reach, seeking raw materials from Africa and North America. In addition, China now permits her people to spend money abroad as tourists.

Corporate Transformation Techniques

A reminder about the three-phase corporate transformation process may be helpful, before viewing Zheng He's actions through that lens.

A company in financial difficulties must turn around from the path it has been following. The three-phase corporate transformation process may be compared to treatinga patient who needs surgery, resuscitation and therapy.

Phase One: Surgery

The surgery phase is to restructure the company to face the new harsh realities. During this phase, it involves cutting costs, improving operational efficiency and seeking a quick increase in cash flow. This may involve reducing headcount, replacing first-class airline flights with conference calls, or selling out-dated goods at a discount (and terminating warehouse leases). This phase is "ruthless" since the corporation's continued existence is at stake. However, it must not be a mindless cost-cutting exercise and improving operational efficiency; it must also prepare the way for the next phases.

This phase requires a surgeon with a scalpel, not a butcher with a cleaver or swordsman with a broadsword. It is not a burn and slash exercise but rather calls for the surgeon's skill. As a surgeon needs a team of nurses, so the turnaround executive needs a team to implement the strategy and to assist in communicating the strategy to the employees. In fact, communication is vital in managing the negative emotions surrounding layoffs or cutbacks. Timely and transparent communications can raise morale, since people will rally around a forthright leader who promises and delivers decisive action. While the management team has a role in communications, the turnaround executive must deliver the top-level news directly to the organization. A doctor does not delegate the task of delivering important information to a nurse to inform the patient; the doctor speaks directly with the patient.

Phase Two: Resuscitation

The resuscitation phase is to revitalise the revenues and the profits. It seeks new markets and new sources of revenue. This phase must set and achieve the short-term goal of returning to profitability. It must balance the cost cutting from the first phase with the need for expanding its market reach and sales revenues.

Some modern corporations are beginning to learn to use digital social media. Even for companies that are not formally going through corporate turnaround, the learning process is like experiencing a resuscitation phase. Facebook and Twitter, whether mediated by computers or smartphone text messaging, call for historically new degrees of honesty, openness, transparency and collaboration with customers. Just one example will suffice: a hotel chain learned of a bedbug incident because a visitor used Twitter to complain to friends. A company must establish an online presence to monitor complaints and deliver its own message.

The company must then be quick to respond and honest in its dealings. Customers will provide feedback; how will the company respond to harsh criticism read by, potentially, hundreds or thousands of interested bystanders?

Simply in terms of marketing, traditional media are saturated and often mistrusted. Building relationships with customers via two-way digital media, like Facebook and Twitter, is one avenue where customers may be found. Another path is to co-brand or co-operate, as found in the alliances between software companies and mobile telephone manufacturers. Microsoft and Google battle each other using Nokia and others as partners.

Phase Three: Therapy

The therapy phase is to rehabilitate a strong and healthy corporate culture. It consolidates previous gains by instilling a new corporate culture that seeks and adapts to new challenges. This phase may introduce revenue sharing or continuous improvement programs; it may seek new ways for employees to cooperate rather than compete. During this phase, the corporate leader must look toward the future and plan for the long-term viability and growth sustainability of the company. This is a phase to build a strong corporate immune culture. In medical science, we understand that the best way to fight viruses is to build a strong immune system. In corporation, the strong corporate immune system is the corporate culture that is fast, flexible and innovative.

The therapy stage is somewhat like the Eastern view of traditional Chinese herbal medicine, which seeks to balance and regulate the flow of energy in the body. Western medicine, by contrast, uses drugs to treat specific ailments, often by killing disease germs. Herbal medicine often takes a longer view, seeking to strengthen the patient by improving internal harmony. Corporate "therapy" must take a long-term view for sustainable growth.

The phase one and to some extent phase 2, sit very well with the western medical system which is ideal to treat acute diseases. The phase three is one that parallels the Chinese traditional medicine to treat chronic diseases.

Selective Techniques or Long-Term Strategy

While the corporate transformation strategy presents the three phases as a sequence of consecutive stages in turning a business around, it may be more useful to view Zheng He as using specific techniques under the right circumstances.

General Electric (GE)'s corporate transformation under CEO Jack Welch provides a modern perspective on the corporate transformation strategy, and also has parallels to the voyages and deeds of Zheng He during the fifteenth-century. Although "Neutron Jack" started transforming GE with great energy in the 1980's, he did not become "transformational" until later in his tenure. During the first phase, or "surgery," Welch pushed his executive team hard enough that they got into legal trouble for polluting New York's Hudson River and also for skirting financial ethics. During this time, Welch may not have been a match for Zheng He as a diplomat.

During the resuscitation and therapy stages, Welch became less aggressive. Some executives would disagree with that assessment, since Welch broke down the corporate feudal structure wherein managers would pursue their own goals within their own divisions, at the expense of corporate development. He also dismantled the financial controls that prohibited most projects, no matter how worthwhile. However, these changes permitted and encouraged collaboration between divisions, a synergy that was of great benefit to the corporation.

"Transformational Jack" emerged towards the end of his career, when he spent a significant amount of time mentoring the next generation of leaders at Crotonville, GE's educational campus. By fostering "the GE way" in passing along the corporate culture to these new managers, Welch more closely emulated Zheng He's development of his diplomatic corps.

Internal or External Transformation

Normally the goal of Corporate Transformation is to save an organization by transforming its mind set and culture. Jack Welch is an excellent example of a leader who transformed his company.

On the other hand, Zheng He's mission was to transform the attitude of China's allies and trading partners, rather than to change China's attitudes towards foreigners or about its own politics or culture. Despite this, some of his methods foreshadowed Corporate Transformation, and his brilliantly collaborative management style can still serve as an example for modern leaders. With this in mind, it is important to remember that Zheng He lived more than five centuries ago. He did not have a formal Corporate Transformation model to follow. Instead, he put his tremendous spirit into his voyages, combining his military insight with the great humanitarian soul he so obviously possessed.

Historical Background for Zheng He

Zhu Di usurped the imperial throne of China in 1403 to become Emperor Yongle. Yongle continued to follow the policies of his predecessor, Emperor Taizu, with regard to foreign relations. These policies could be summarized as: defend Chinese borders against incursion; maintain peaceful and friendly relations with neighbouring countries; and encourage foreign trade, including the receipt of tribute from allied nations.

China's most important international commerce had included selling tea, spices, silk and ceramics. Trade routes included overland caravans and ocean-going trade. Since ceramics were heavier than spices, these goods were better suited to transportation by ship.

Emperor Yongle made one change, however. He promoted trade by means of pro-active diplomacy. His probable motive was to firmly establish himself as the internationally recognized emperor of China; but the method would strengthen both diplomatic and trade relationships with a large number of other countries. He assigned these tasks to Zheng He.

Admiral Zheng He made seven grand voyages; the first six for Emperor Yongle. Yongle's son halted these expeditions, but the subsequent Emperor XuanZong sent Zheng He on one more. Between one hundred and two hundred ships were involved in each voyage.

A typical visit from Zheng He would include:

- A public proclamation of the Emperor's mission statement
- Official visits with the local ruler, including an exchange of gifts
- Provision of medical treatment to the local populace, by the fleet's medical cadre
- Enforcement of law, by capturing pirates who preyed upon either the Chinese or the local traders

Despite the success of his missions, Zheng He did not become the first in a line of ambassadors for China. Subsequent emperors changed China's attitude from a policy of open and frequent contact with foreign powers, to one of severe isolationism that lasted about five centuries.

However, China has recently emerged from its "bamboo curtain" with a renewed interest in international commerce. Some have heard echoes of Zheng He's approach in these new ventures.

Zheng He: Collaboration and Cooperation, Rather than War

Zheng He stood in contrast to Sun Zi (or Sun Tzu or Sun Wu) who is famous for writing The Art of War. Sun Zi emphasized defeating an enemy. Knowledge and force were vital in gaining victory.

Zheng He, on the other hand, served an emperor who pursued diplomatic relations, peace and prosperity through commerce. Zheng He collaborated with foreign leaders. He won their cooperation through honesty and openness.

It can be argued that Zheng He did indeed start from a position of strength. It must have been unsettling for a ruler to see an armada of over one hundred ships arrive for a visit from one's most powerful neighbour. But even when Zheng He commanded his largest fleet of 200 ships, they did not loot, pillage or conquer. His major pursuits were diplomacy, collaboration and commerce, never military conquest.

Sun Zi lived and fought in sixth-century China, prior to its unification from competing nation-states. In contrast, Zheng He was a cosmopolitan traveller, well acquainted with a variety of different cultures.

Although politicians and business moguls might use Sun Zi's The Art of War, it was written primarily for military purposes. While Zheng He had military clout, as an admiral in command of a large fleet of ships, his concern was diplomacy and commerce. Zheng He did not conquer or occupy the countries he visited, nor did he annex them to China. Indeed, his memory is still honoured in a number of those countries, by means of monuments, relics and historical writings.

Sun Zi may have been a contemporary of Confucius; some recommend studying The Art of War from a Taoist viewpoint. Zheng He's religious views, on the other hand, may have incorporated Islam.

Modern business is sometimes regarded as cut-throat competition, and the win-lose paradigm is often invoked. There may be greater wisdom, however, in seeking win-win encounters. Games theory shows that, in many cases, long-term cooperation can yield better results than ruthless competition.

With the Internet, and the spectre that Wikileaks might expose corporate as well as diplomatic secrets, business organizations should emphasize sharing information in a way that leads to mutual advantage.

Games theory explores some interesting situations where cooperation yields a better result than competition. The "Prisoners' Dilemma" is well known. If one prisoner betrays the other, the result is better for the betrayer and worse for the other. If both prisoners stay loyal to each other, they receive a minor punishment. However, if each betrays the other, the result is very poor for both. The best long-term strategy, if the two players will "play the game" several times, is to remain loyal. Only in a one-time situation might one person benefit by betraying the other. One is unlikely to take over a rival through one marketing campaign, so it makes sense to plan for the long term. It is even less wise to bankrupt a supplier or customer by entering into a lopsided contract. Therefore Zheng He's cooperative approach is more suited to business in the modern-day globalised era than Sun Zi's competitive style.

Zheng He is an Example for Collaborative Corporate Transformation

Zheng He was not a business executive, saving a corporation from bankruptcy. He did, however, use many of the techniques espoused by the Corporate Transformation in its three phases of surgery, resuscitation, and therapy. A summary of the corporate transformation used by Zheng He is depicted in the appendix (case study 1).

Although Corporate Transformation does progress from one stage to the next, Zheng He used the techniques at different times and according to his immediate circumstances and needs. Zheng He also used a more collaborative style than would be expected for his times...or even in modern times.

Zheng He and Surgery Techniques

To use "Surgery" techniques requires a leader who is bold and resolute. Clear directions must be given, and the leader must ensure that orders are carried out. The situation requires decisive measures, because failure in this stage spells the end of the mission.

Zheng He used "Surgery" techniques in two ways: in preparation and in law enforcement.

The Surgery of Preparation

Serious, careful and meticulous planning is required to sail a fleet of over a hundred vessels. Trade goods, provisions and labour are obvious pre-requisites; but so are plans for the weather and ports for layovers and repairs.

Zheng He received explicit instructions from the Emperor as to which countries to visit. Zheng He then had to ensure that ports were ready for ships to dock; that repair facilities would be available; and that there would be land available for temporary warehouses.

Even more in the fifteenth-century than today, ocean travel depended on the weather. Zheng He made use of monsoon winds to power his sails; this required timing the visits and planning on layovers when the winds would not blow his way. His voyages typically took two years, based on the weather conditions.

As one example of staffing: the fleet employed one medic for every 150 or so sailors and staff personnel. The medical team treated the masses at each port of call, as part of Zheng He's diplomatic overtures.

Zheng He and the emperor also ensured that he had a team of high-level envoys who were deployed on side missions during the voyage. With the right staff available, Zheng He could leverage his abilities. This is an obvious parallel to the way of a surgeon who leads the surgical team: anaesthesiologist, anaesthetist, scrub nurse, circulating nurse etc.

Zheng He had to keep a relentless focus while preparing for each voyage. He had to remain on top of details, and to insist on results. In command of up to 27,000 people, Zheng He could not afford wasted efforts or delays.

In such a large operation, delegation of authority and responsibility is paramount for success. Zheng He led his team by giving them opportunities to learn, to take responsibility, and to make preparations for their roles in the voyages.

Actually Emperor Yongle had prepared the way for Zheng He, by sending out a reconnaissance voyage two years before Zheng He's first. No doubt Zheng He learned from, and improved upon, the Emperor's preparations for that mission.

Zheng He also used a continuous improvement process. He deliberately found ways to improve on his team's operational efficiency after each voyage. This was especially important because many of his men were soldiers, medics or diplomats, not sailors. As an example, his first voyage did not visit nearly as many countries as subsequent voyages. They could learn from the first voyage and apply those lessons to the later ones.

The Surgery of Law Enforcement

During his voyages, Zheng He also arrested several pirate bands that had been identified by the emperor. This is an obvious case where decisive action was required. By ridding the waters of these pirates, particularly at the Strait of Malacca, Zheng He created safe passage through the straits, as well as increasing Ming status in Southeast Asia.

It is essential to note that Zheng He was careful to maintain good relations, both with the local rulers and with the emperor, while performing his policing duties. He had to avoid antagonizing the locals or harming innocent bystanders. Like any CEO, he had to ensure that the Chairman had the final verdict in dealing with captured pirates.

Had Zheng He dealt with the pirates without first gaining the approval of the local rulers, his police actions could have been seen as aggression against them. Had he executed the pirates, the Emperor would have been deprived of his opportunity to exercise justice. In collaborating with his Emperor and with the local authorities, Zheng He advanced his primary mission of fostering good will and respect for the Chinese among the people he visited.

In both roles, as a planner and as an agent of law enforcement, Zheng He demonstrated a corporate surgeon's precision in planning details, clarity of instruction to subordinates, and resolute diligence in acting.

Zheng He and Resuscitation Techniques

"Resuscitation" shifts the focus from the immediate to the medium term. It builds on past success from the "Surgery" phase. In a corporate setting, cash flow would still be critical, however building the future cannot come at the expense of current revenue.

Clearly Zheng He was a master of resuscitation techniques, as shown in five areas: developing markets; expert salesmanship; public relations; serving customers' interests; and making investments.

Resuscitation through Developing Markets

Zheng He "developed new business" by going to his "customers." He found new opportunities by strengthening old ties with neighbouring countries. This push for new and expanded markets is in keeping with the corporate resuscitation phase.

A major part of Zheng He's work could be considered "resuscitation." It did look to the past, since an element of the mission was to remind the neighbouring states that they needed to maintain friendly relations with China. Although he definitely expended most of his effort in expanding commerce with markets that were already known to the Chinese, he was expanding China's economic reach by changing these neighbours from quiet bystanders into active trading partners.

Resuscitation through Expert Salesmanship

On his fourth mission, for example, Zheng He took 63 ships and over 27,000 men to the Maldives, Hormuz and Aden. As a result of this journey, nineteen countries sent return missions to the Ming capital at Nanking, a real coup for Zheng He in terms of market development. Zheng He accompanied the representatives of these missions back to their home countries as part of his fifth expedition.

This was a significant act of cooperation and support. Zheng He's naval capabilities were superior to those of the countries he visited. Zheng He had to coordinate these foreign vessels along with his own fleet, expending his effort, but making the trip much safer for his allies.

Resuscitation through Public Relations

Whenever Zheng He dealt directly with agents from different countries or cultures, he would have been very aware of the public relations role he was taking on. He was representing the Emperor at all times, and in essence, was acting as a salesman for China: he was selling the goodwill and culture of his home country, intending that the host country would "buy" what was on offer and open trade relations with China.

Resuscitation through Serving Customers' Interests

All those actions contributed to Zheng He's resuscitation techniques. He eliminated territorial struggles by providing the conduit for envoys from neighbouring countries to visit China and return home safely. This was a clear instance of integrated diversity and countries sharing in a common vision: the value of maintaining friendly and open trade relationships. Taking action to further their joint interests was another example of the collaborative spirit Zheng He brought to all these dealings.

Resuscitation through Making Investments

His missions did require a significant investment from the Chinese, in building the ships and facilities such as warehouses and shipyards. However, Zheng He had an obligation to "make a profit" during his voyages, in terms of building goodwill, earning respect, and of course in the commercial trade in which his team was engaged. In this sense, Zheng He was involved in the "Resuscitation" phase. He was building toward the future while still making it pay off during the present.

Zheng He and Therapy Techniques

In Corporate Transformation, the "Therapy" phase begins to develop a new mind set and a new corporate culture. These are essential for the long-term growth of the company, although they will not, by themselves, save a company from bankruptcy. The "Therapy" phase requires a more collaborative leadership style than the one used in "Surgery."

Zheng He provided therapy by using creative innovation and planning for sustainable growth. He empowered his subordinates, spread goodwill and planned for the future. However, the main intent was to change the other countries, not the Chinese themselves. His goal was to improve China's standing among the foreign countries, by demonstrating goodwill and collaboration. It was incidental that his work could have led to further changes among the Chinese, had later Emperors followed the path of Emperor Yongle.

Therapy by Empowering Subordinates

Admiral Zheng He developed and commanded a very large fleet. He delegated diplomatic missions to his subordinates, arranging for later rendezvous, and co-ordinated their efforts. This is similar to the way a manager at any level might provide growth opportunities for his or her direct reports. This is a clear example of empowering his "employees." The advantage of this empowerment is the upgrading of an employee's attitude and performance as they take "ownership" of their responsibilities and duties. Another bonus to empowerment is the increase of innovation and creativity from an individual. When one feels free to work on their own, there is a freedom in how they relate to the company or employer. This freedom often results in a surge of creativity, a plus for the company, and certainly a large benefit to the employee.

Therapy by Spreading Goodwill

Remember that, as an admiral, Zheng He could have used military might to impress and influence his foreign neighbours. By using the soft power of trade, and restraining his fleet from military action, Zheng He was beginning to change the attitudes of the foreign leaders.

Although the policy of developing trading

partnerships was not new in China, Zheng He did work hard to push the foreign leaders into this mindset. This is like the corporate therapy phase that fosters change in one's own corporate culture. A very specific example was making the Chinese medics available to as many people as possible in each port of call. This demonstrated that the Chinese had something to offer, even beyond trade goods.

Therapy by Planning for the Future

The above actions are like building a new corporate culture. The other aspect of the therapy stage of the three-phase transformation program is to make long-term plans and initiate the actions to make them a reality. Zheng He worked toward this goal, by concentrating his later voyages not on law enforcement, but on the continuation of the new trade relations that were in place. Zheng He was obviously aware that maintaining the goodwill that had been established on his earlier voyages was as important as law enforcement, perhaps even more important. People like to feel as though they are important and are partners in a relationship, rather than subjects that need to be ruled with an iron fist. This may have continued indefinitely and sustained long term growth, but before Zheng He could start out on his seventh voyage, Emperor Yongle died, and the next emperor changed the strategic direction for China. Yongle's grandson reinstated the diplomatic voyages, largely because no tribute had been received for several years. Zheng He served on only one voyage for XuanZong; no further voyages were made for centuries.

Five centuries later, the new Chinese aspiration to become a significant player in the global economy may be traced back to Zheng He's voyages. Modern China is generating goodwill and investing heavily in Africa and Latin America, helping the troubled European countries with sovereign debt problems and sending Chinese tourists all over the world including its erstwhile enemy Taiwan. China even extended a helping hand to quake-stricken Japan, even though there were diplomatic rows for a short period of time. It is winning the goodwill of the world through spreading economic goodwill. This is contrary to the US, which is bogged down and hasgenerated a lot of problems with military incursions into Iraq and Afghanistan.

General Electric, Admiral Zheng He and Corporate Transformation

In the early 1980s General Electric Corporation (GE) applied corporate transformation techniques to transform itself into an economic powerhouse. GE was already large, but it required serious and lasting changes. Jack Welch became Chairman and CEO in 1981 and began making those changes. A summary of the corporate transformation strategies used by Jack Welch is shown below in the appendix (case study 2).

Although Welch was not Chinese, his approach to improving GE used techniques found in both the yet-to-be-invented Corporate Transformation strategy and the methods Zheng He used in opening up trade for China.

GE's Surgery Phase: Operational Productivity

Perhaps the most daring change Welch introduced at GE was to "de-layer" the company. He had long believed that its many layers of management fostered bureaucratic timidity rather than innovation and productivity. Part of that bureaucracy was a "financial mafia" that controlled spending so tightly that it choked reinvestment. Decreasing the layers of management bureaucracy allowed for more freedom to reinvest. Welch also reduced inventory levels dramatically.

GE's new strategy was to become either #1 or #2 in any given market; or to exit that market altogether. The company sold off divisions that did not lead their markets. This reduced staff and simplified the corporate structure. Welch focussed on high growth while shrinking the head office division.

Staff learned to accept that low-performing employees would lose their jobs; the target was about a 5% annual dismissal rate. Another cultural change was that simplicity would eventually triumph over bureaucracy.

By shedding both low-performing employees and uncompetitive divisions, Welch demonstrated the intense, ruthless focus on cost-saving measures that are characteristic of the Surgery phase.

Emperor Yongle had set Zheng He the task of strengthening foreign trade while demonstrating

Yongle's power and emphasizing the legitimacy of his rule, including defeating the pirate chief, Chen Zuyi, in order to maintain order along maritime routes. Admiral Zheng He amassed a huge fleet and made his plans with a strict attention to detail. Zheng He ensured that his armada would be well prepared, and also well disciplined to ensure the Emperor's orders would be carried out. Zheng He had three methods to guarantee the success of his tasks. Like Jack Welch of GE, Zheng He focused upon three main principles:

- Simplicity
- The goal to become number one
- Strategic planning.

The simplicity of Zheng He's voyages was apparent in the map of his travels. He did not attempt to explore unknown countries; China was aware of the majority of countries surrounding the Indian Ocean, and had been, for centuries, a primary producer and consumer of goods trading between the Mediterranean, African and Middle Eastern.

He also endeavoured **to** become number one at what he did. With the Emperor's financial and ideological support, plus his own military acumen, it is not difficult to understand how he became the legend of the sea, a distinction that still holds true today.

His strategic planning included arranging for large numbers of sailors, huge ships, and carefully premeditated ports of call. This meticulous planning was critical in making all of his voyages an overwhelming success.

One other aspect used by Zheng He was his recognition of his men, as well as other cultures and people within their own right. He respected the men under his command, and, in turn received their respect. There would be no other way to command up to 27,000 men over an immense armada of ships. Likewise, his esteem and reverence for the foreign societies that he visited helped to make China (and Zheng He himself) a popular, yet formidable force.

By undertaking a long-range approach, Zheng He prepared the way for numerous journeys that would become as successful as his first.

The characteristics shared by Zheng He and Jack Welch was the demonstration of laser-like focus and intensity during the early stages of their tenure as the top leaders of their organizations.

GE's Resuscitation Phase: Productivity with Innovation

GE's resuscitation phase began a turn toward innovation. Product innovation was made possible by eliminating "turf wars" between divisions; the company began to eliminate internal boundaries. Divisions shared knowledge on best practices, such as Six Sigma and work-out.

GE's strategy shifted toward integrated diversity in its teams and products. Cross-functioning teamwork meant that people with various skills and backgrounds would work together on a project, rather than reviewing and criticizing other divisions' projects.
Welch pushed the corporation to pursue common goals, rather than allowing each division to focus on success for itself at the expense of others.

One innovation made by Zheng He was the inclusion of medical staff in his fleet. These doctors worked to keep his sailors healthy, and also served foreigners in each port of call. Their medical aid was effective in building goodwill, trust and cooperation in each country they visited. When Zheng He shared his doctor's medical expertise with the populace in his various ports, he was removing obstacles to establishing good diplomatic relations with the people of these countries.

Zheng He's fleet also included specialists in languages, commerce, construction, and of course sailing. These cross-function teams were essential for communication with the people they visited. Zheng He knew that the Chinese would have to buy and sell, to build warehouses, and to travel from place to place safely, and the most productive way for this to happen was by establishing distinct political interactions within each destination he visited.

GE's elimination of internal boundaries worked in much the same way. Welch understood that advancement was not possible as long as the company was battling itself internally. By encouraging the pursuit of more efficient practices, including cutting back on inventories and taking apart the bureaucracy that was performing inadequately. As Zheng He learned, Jack Welch also realised that the strength of any company relies upon the individuals that make up its constituency. By encouraging innovation and cooperation within their respective organizations, both Zheng He and Jack Welch were able to successfully communicate and manage those subordinate to them.

GE's Therapy Phase: Continuous Innovation

Welch then pushed GE to adopt a cycle of continuous innovation. Rather than running a product through a "develop, then sell until the competition catches up" timeline, GE would continue improving products or developing replacements. As well, new systems and methodologies were introduced so GE could innovate more while consuming fewer resources.

Part of the strategy was to empower employees, so decisions could be made farther down the corporate ladder. Flexibility, rather than bureaucracy, was rewarded.

Two of the cultural changes were the "360-degree appraisal" and the "Crotonville-GE way." The first involves performance appraisal by peers, subordinates and customers as well as by managers. The second refers to GE's educational campus, which embodies the goal of life-long learning.

Zheng He also "empowered" his diplomatic staff. He sent them on missions, trusting that they had the skills to succeed even when he was not present. Of course, they did rendezvous later so he was kept informed after the missions. These were learning opportunities for his subordinates, who were nonetheless responsible for their missions.

It does seem a pity that Zheng He's work was not continued by the next Emperor; it would have been interesting to see how Chinese culture could have developed with further cultural and ideological exchange. By turning inward after Zheng He's missions, China was unable to create the major culture shift that GE would experience under the leadership of Jack Welch centuries later. Following the death of Emperor Yongle in 1424, the Ming dynasty temporarily put an end to its attempts to establish subsidiary states and economic partners throughout Southeast Asia. When Emperor Yongle's grandson ascended the throne, Zheng He began his seventh and final voyage; however, advocates for an isolationist foreign policy held sway, and the funding for Zheng He's enormous undertakings was withdrawn. Rather than utilizing the corporate transformation techniques, as General Electric did about550 years later, China allowed the great strides made by Zheng He to fall by the wayside.

Both Zheng He and Jack Welch worked to change their organizational cultures. Zheng He laid the foundation for future trade and international relations, but China did not follow through for five centuries. Jack Welch succeeded in making the changes he envisioned for the corporate culture at GE, especially in making lifelong learning a key part of an employee's career.

The Timeless Nature of Corporate Transformation Techniques

Zheng He in the fifteenth-century, and Jack Welch in the twentieth, all applied the techniques of corporate transformation in their own situations. Each achieved spectacular success as leaders in challenging circumstances. Zheng He and Jack Welch led large hierarchical organizations.

Allof these men demonstrated that collaboration, teamwork and cooperation are powerful tools of leadership. Zheng He strengthened alliances with foreign leaders, people who may have distrusted or feared China's might. Jack Welch overturned vested interests inside General Electric, leading to cooperation from aptly-named corporate "divisions."

The same techniques can be, and have been, applied in a number of corporations in recent decades. The three-phase corporate transformation program provides a way forward through difficulties to success. Jack Welch has confirmed using the transformational strategies successfully. Zheng He was indeed a great corporate transformation expert and inspiration, and used the transformation strategies much earlier. He had paved the way for the globalisation success of modern day China.

Appendix
CASE STUDY 1 – ZHENG HE AND THE THREE PHASES

	Surgery	Resuscitation	Therapy
Operation	Preparation Law Enforcement	Salesmanship Customer First	Positive Trade Cross Cultural Relations
Strategy	Carefully select countries to visit Build (Shipyards)	Public Relations Build more Infrastructure (Warehouses)	Plan for future Bring foreign people home
Culture	Increase Commerce Avoid War	Develop Friendly Relationships Adventurism	Em-power workers Medical care for foreign people

CASE STUDY 2: USE OF THREE PHASES BY GENERAL ELECTRIC

	Surgery	Resuscitation	Therapy
Operation	De-layering Dismantle "Financial Mafia" More with less	Eliminate turf wars No boundaries Best practices (six sigma)	Product development Innovation with less New systems
Strategy	No 1 or 2 High growth Shrink HQ Strategic planning	Integrated diversity Cross-Functional teamwork	Empowerment: Decision making at lower levels Reward flexibility
Culture	Simplicity Fire bottom 5%	Shared vision and values Work out	360 degree appraisal Crotonville – GE Way

REFERENCES

Hoon, Hum Sin and Chew Lusheng Grace. *"The Art of Collaboration: A Management Perspective Drawn From the Grand Voyages of Admiral Zheng He."* NUS, Business School, June 2010.

Sen, Tan Ta. *"Cheng Ho and Cultural Exchange in the Context of Southeast Asia."*

Teng, Michael ,*"Corporate Turnaround: Nursing a sick company back to health"*, Prentice Hall, 2002

Teng. Michael, *"Training Manual: Corporate Turnaround and Transformation"*, Corporate Turnaround Centre Pte Ltd, 2008

Teng. Michael, *"Toolkit: Corporate Transformation to improve productivity and innovation"*, Corporate Turnaround Centre Pte Ltd, 2010

Teng, Michael, *"Ancient Chinese Wisdom Transform Your Business: Lessons from Zheng He, Confucius and Sun Zi,* Corporate Turnaround Centre Pte Ltd, 2014

www.ingramcontent.com/pod-product-compliance
Lightning Source LLC
Chambersburg PA
CBHW070714180526
45167CB00004B/1473